Upstream Gold

Upstream Gold
Cyle Salmon

Upstream Gold
© 2025 Cyle Salmon
ISBN: 979-8-9987811-3-1

Published by Youth Writer's Press
Colton, California
youthwriterspress.com

First Edition, 2025

To request permissions, you may contact the Publisher at
info@youthwriterscamp.com

Printed in the United States of America.

Cover design by Cyle Salmon & Emily Anne Evans
Layout design by Emily Anne Evans / Photon Moment LLC

To my mom and dad for always supporting my dreams.
I love and appreciate you both more than you could know.

To you, the readers, for supporting one of the
stepping stones toward a lifelong goal—
I couldn't do it without you!

Contents

Foreword

A life of sudden storms and shifting paths has forged our son, Cyle, just as Damascus Steel is forged — layer upon layer, each one hammered by fire and trial, each one adding to its unmatched strength and beauty. So has Cyle been shaped by life's wild turns, emerging unbent, unbroken, and wondrously rare.

Struggle is no stranger to anyone; the trials that shape life's course touch all in time. Many wear masks, concealing the places where emotional pain has bitten deep, softening the edges with a smile for themselves and for those they cherish. Yet some burdens stand in plain sight, unhidden and undeniable. In such moments, one must stand firm, meeting them with grit, with steadfast will, and with tireless resolve. Naturally, one is shaped as Damascus Steel is shaped — each challenge folded into the weave of character, each hardship pressed into the layers of being, until strength and resilience shine forth, both visible and enduring.

The poems in this collection are his truth made tangible. They come from the depths of his soul, each word a piece of his heart, each verse a layer forged from experience and growth. Within these pages, he has poured raw emotion, hard-earned wisdom, and the kind of honesty that can only be forged through trial. These poems do more than tell his story — they hold a mirror for anyone who has faced their own storms, an invitation to look within, to dig deep, and to discover the strength that waits to be uncovered.

We are proud beyond measure of the courage he shows in revealing his journey, and of the person he has become — and continues to become — with each passing day. May his words inspire you, as his life inspires us, to stand unbent, unbroken, and wondrously rare.

Cyle: We cherish the honor of calling you our son.

Love,
Mom and Dad

Upstream Gold

Who am I?

I'm Cyle Salmon
A fish that swims upstream for the simple things
A fish who's been cut and setback more times than the
scales on his back
A fish that was burnt and tossed out
by the self-proclaimed Angel fish
A fish that left the reef to go to the trenches to die
A fish that got left out like a boring ol' clownfish
At least, that's what the sharks shout.

I'm Cyle Salmon
Yes I swim upstream for the nice things.
Yes I've been cut, burnt and thrown out by the
high and mighty.
But I keep it goin',
for all the fishies to one day see
The burns keep the steel hot, ready to be forged once
more into somethin' sharper and stronger
The cuts just preppin' the scales makin' em harder for
the next ones
Till one day ain't nobody tryna cut no more.

And when I'm thrown out by the high and mighty,

I keep it goin'

Cause I'm Cyle Salmon

That's what I shout.

Golden

The currents been pushin me down, keepin' me full of hesitation.

All the other schools been whisperin' bout how if there were no sharks, they'd be done by now.

But it ain't the sharks keepin' the 99 down.

It's the 99s dead coral crowns of past hopes and present fears.

Cause from every light the Kingfish strikes, as the 99 parry's the same gift giving light.

Every wake against the current the kingfish bleeds at hardship

While the 99 tryna' sidestep the process

But hey, when the kingfish is hard and golden, they just some lucky jo.

My fins ache at the 99 tryna get around the sharks in the currents

Cause I'm tryna get golden.

Ain't nothin golden come from the 99 'cept the disses and rumors they be spittin.'

But the 99 be holdin me around keepin' me down with their "preppin'."

My fins yearn for the currents and sharks out there
Cause I'm tryna get golden.
My fins yearn for the kingfish's gold and toughness
but is dragged, by the 99s preppin.'

The Kind Man

Everything was blooming,

Everything was bright.

The rivers rushin and pushin.

The fins on my back, energetic and powerful as my
bears claw.

The scales across my back harder than an iron net of the
dark gods

Then it all died in the wisp of a current,

The waters turned black as the kind man died,

The darkness brought wounds of all shapes and sizes,

Then the rivers turned rapid as the heavens turned
mountains.

The water turned thinner than the gills along my back.

Than pranced the kind man's daughter prancing along
the school keeping the darkness away

Then came the kind man's sister remedying the slashes
and gashes,

Once she healed she taught her way to keep the
darkness away with the simple things,

Once the journey was over lightning rang and turned the
darkness away.

The heavens turned back the mountains and made the
rapids clear way.
The kind man's sister then left knowing we were okay,
but the school left her ways behind.
Time passed and the kind man's daughter slowly moved
away,
The kind man's daughter smiled at me the morning the
light took her away.
Later that season her ashes rained from the storm.
The kind man's life remains and shows the way,
Through the flames do I rise from darkness,
Through the water I breath do I keep it away,
The kind man's life remains and shows us the way.

Imperfect Me

I used to be 9 at body and mind,

Now I am me.

I used to be an extension of my emotions, of depressions

internal waves and caves,

Now I am me.

I used to be lazy, hardly doing anything when there is so

much to be done,

Now I am me.

I used to be what other schools told me to be,

Now I am me.

I used to be many things,

But now, I am me.

I used to be wrong,

Now I am continuing to be wrong

but now as the new me.

I used to be stagnant in the waves of life and death,

Now I am learning how to be a new me while surfing the

very same waves.

I used to want gold,

Now I want to be the golden new me.

I used to want others growth and positions,

Now I want to water me for the new me,

so I can be me.

I used to want so many things,

But that was not me, so now I water my own me.

I used to be discontent with myself, layin' on the ground
doin nothin with it,

Now I take it and use it as the blueprint for the new me.

I used to let my storms decide my direction, like a tale of
an old king,

Now the storms are under my reign as a mighty
warsteed.

I used to be the injured, crippled and hopeless,

Now I dream of the new me being the light shining into
the oceans of others.

I used to try and stop the change only looking two steps
ahead seeing the darkness,

Now the new me looks back and sees the heavens'
plans.

This is why I look forward to the golden new me pouring
into millions of oceans, lakes, pounds and puddles.

The old me is good, the new me will be golden, But today I am me learning and growing with the water and light I let in from the heavens.

Mighty Warsteed

Run,

Run now,

Run as fast as you can from the darkness around you

Run hard every day not towards success but from the
shadowy night

Success is a fairy tale the mothers whisper at lightfall

The bear is a darkness the devil sent during the
grandfathers ring

It stalks and it stalks until you wear from the restless
nights and blinding lights

The eyes weigh upon you like the iron nets guilt that
took you away but left you behind

Its claws strike in five separate motions not for the drip
of the blood but for the slip of a fall

Its first claw shines only to inflict fear controlling your
mind

The second uses the control and steers you towards the
cliffside

You scream and you struggle but the darkness is around
you, In you, is you

The third is now done making you panic gifting control when there was nothing yet to fear
The fourth fills old space of dreams and love with ocean blue leeches

...

This is my fear, the bear in the dark with five separate claws,
It stalks and it stalks waiting until I create it.
It uses the schools rumors as nightly feasts of satisfaction,
It morphs as I grow becoming what I tell it, but yet at times I do not know it.

But yet do I fear the bear or does the bear fear me?
Does it hunt for satisfaction or safety?
Does it keep me from the nets or simply keep me for its games?
I do not know my bear and my bear may not know me
But I am my bear and my bear is part of me so I ride it like the current of a rapid as my mighty warsteed

Class VI

"Carefull now!" The ferryman shouts.
The yacht purrs as the party roars over the old man,
smoothly drifting over the calm waters.
The air breezes, soft as a mothers touch, refreshing as
laughter.
As they drift farther they soon become Martyr's,
None take heed as all are now fodder.

The party boat grinds as the wine gets lost in time
The sun sets and the boats' sealed in memories shrine
The spiders climb as they are webbing and weaving
deaths ancient old rhymes,
The boat unfit for the currents docked in a lonely old. line
All are blind to fates' design.

The great horned owls now peering down on those who
have be sworn to drown
The moon now up dancing with the wolves at the crown.
The canoers begin to murmur and frown,
"Somthings not right..." Oh what bad clowns!

The river swishes and swashes all the way down until the water is as white as the last minutes of snowdown.

The lightning cracks and burns through the stormy night sky
The raft held by hopes and dreams slowly losing space, making the mother cry,
The wolves howl and the moon flies high shining a spotlight on tonight's cream pies
One hit of the rock and the family now crashes from modern days high,
All now separated, all now lost, in the one place no one escapes from themself.

This is the rapid the salmon tours daily,
This is my river and millions of others,
We look bright and quiet on the river's entrance, but our ferrymans warned it was a class six by the exit.
Our rivers are our minds, calm on the outside, boiling and overflowing with emotion deep inside.

"Carefull now!" ringing through the minds of the warned that chose to ignore.

A Violent Tide

One week before race day

"GO!"

200s kill, regret kills harder.

Our legs crash like waves against the beach,

Pain is temporary, so are our primes.

"16!"

Target locked, thoughts controlled, legs heated.

"33!"

Rep done, 7 to go. Heads racing like a horse

in the open fields.

200s kill, regret kills harder...

"GO!"

One day before race day

"Good to go boys!"

"5 miles there and back, recovery pace! Remember!"

The conversation sparked likes our dreams in Poseidon's

deep dark seas

Dog park was steep, so were our paces, but so were our

dreams,

We were a herd, brothers through the darkness and

light.

The first step is known to be the hardest, but it's the
second mile that bites.
We forged our lungs from steel for the heated trips to our
dreams.
We cruised out as a pack, we cruised in as a pack. One.
Step. Closer.
The acid in our legs packed harder as our legs stretched
farther.
Coaches spaghetti every night brought us all closer.
Closer to each other, closer to our fiery heavens.
"Good to go boys!"

One hour before 1600m
"Go."
The clouds were beginning to thicken,
Our legs shook as the earth,
Not from the nerves of our own,
But from the tridents tips against our throats.
As our legs reached for our youth,
Our hands reached for their death.
The winds carried force in our silence.
The tide has been brought back,
Oh, who will ever survive this violent tide?
"Go"

1600m start line

"GO!!!!"

BANG

Our feet roared

Just as poseidon storms

100Ms done.

place found

Race pace settling

Heads clear

legs fresh

spikes clashing

200Ms done.

Race pace found and following

400Ms done.

Heads fuzzy, but the goal is clear

800Ms done.

Ha- half way...

Lungs being tested

Heads starting to question

Legs going through it

1200Ms done.

Just... trying... to... keep up.

Mind is gone

Eyes heavy

Legs tapping

1500Ms done.

Eyes shut

Legs pounding

One.

Last.

Sprint.

5:15... I'm on the ground.

"Go"

Tyrant's Silence

Tick tock

The core shines bright

The revolution shouts hard torn bites,

But the tyrant masks his warted grasp

Choking the rags out from the dirt into our personal
trash.

One soul at a time cleansed from the earth, adding red
to its hardened clasp

Claiming he's a savior,

healing our kingdom's festering gash.

Tick tock,

Will our throats last?

Snap crack

The tyrant's golden legion parades out back

My family's hearts filled with nightmarish black

Our futures dimmed like a candle running out of wax

Like a heartbeat our voices rise before running out of
slack

All consequence of our attempt to raise an axe at the
tyrant's demoralizing tax,

If only our brothers and sisters would kickback, and take

power back

Snap crack,

Will our throats last?

Thud ump, thud ump

The tyrant slams his cold iron gauntlet

Commanding his squadrons to turn the ground scarlet!

Thud ump, thud ump

My tongue whispers balance but the crowds demand

violence!

Thud ump, thud ump

The blades shred silence.

Thud ump-

Voices now silent.

Thud-

Silent as our society is dormant.

. . .

Burning Tómr

Wake up...

Wake up.

WAKE UP!

My body rises from the drowned's silent cries

I'm alive, but my senses scream that it's all a lie

I pry inside but only an abyss lies

I stare out at the war torn scene for my mind

But it's my heart and soul who continue to cry

"It's time to leave!" The captain decries, the thundering echoing his commanding pleas

The enemies blades sing as the lightning dances to our chorus of screams

I sprint through the night leaving life's strife far and creeping

While my heart sits in spite it continues to root through my empty spaces,

I slow and I slow until my bears are able lash out with a self created snare,

The dozens of eyes whisper, "Chained with no anchor, chained to its own snare."

They devour without churning, but claw as if my world is burning.

But I have no world inside of me.

So they burn where my world was, they burn space.

I tell myself it shouldn't burn... but it does.

And it burns. So. Bad.

That night I cried steaming tears to sleep,

From the fire burning inside of me but leaving me be.

The bears leave me in life but stalk me in sleep.

Until the Alpha bear, tómr, whispers its time to wake.

My eyes flush with life and its vengeance

body hardened with past foes' blood.

My blood.

I'm anchored by the abyss and pry inside but find no

space,

Only my life.

My heart who anchors through the storms

My soul who grows through the wars

My armor who gains sturdiness through the family's lore

And my axe who cuts with more strength each hit that I

pour.

The fire rages from the nights core

Not consuming, only surging

Surging through my wings as I fly towards the war

Bringing my axe down to get back to my North star.

Through each of our North stars do we gain the ability to
soar.
Else we are a husk eaten not by the bear
But our inability to be restored.
Will you soar?

STORM

The storm had arrived, shadowing the king's spark.

Not a soul could forecast nor tame this behemoth.

Not the shamans nor the priests, nor the angels of his

arc

The clouds would crickle and crackle until they were

fueled by his heart sunken monolith,

Striking down on the seeking king, relieving him of his

royal bark.

It strikes and it strikes fueled by his emotion "I won't stay

down. . ." he oaths.

It strikes throughout the night every time with utter

starkness.

Knowing that he fuels its wrath,

Knowing he is his own shark.

Only known by what swims in his dark.

Throughout the night the aspiring king must go through

his pain,

Without one's own conquering of personal stains

How would they sustain?

The morning rises and the king has been all but drained,

"Let us tame our own storm!" He has not been slain!

That night the preyed king kneels to pray

The monolith fuels the storm as it comes to sight

The crimson lightning ignites

But the King exclaims, "I AM NO LONGER YOUR PREY!"

The sunken monolith was full of blight

It is time to give it light

My god has given her rays!

Kingdom delight!

As our strom bites

The storms fray

So let us repay

For today is simple wet clay

And tomorrow is a glorious buffet

For after the storm, life shall parlay

But then my storm rained ashes as the king frantically

tried to repay

Storms never stay...

But they also never go away,

"Rest in peace, STORM!" The king exclaimed!

Who are you?

"Why do you stand there?

Why do you sleep there?

Why do you eat here?

Why do you give them the glare?

Why?

Why?

Why?

Why?

WHY?!?"

That's what the little man in my soul likes to scream...

I look at the ferryman with dread in my eyes

Only met with the most sympathetic of advice,

He tried so I could stop my lies

Told me to stretch

Told me its okay to cry

Told me to try to fly

Even if I failed

And failed

And failed

Told me to just, try

Right up until the day that I die

Try to be kind

Try to be generous

Try to be fun

Try to be… me.

Not the black suits or sly lies

Not me in a societal filters

But the me in this hard torn life

The me I know me to be

The me god gave to me

Cause if I ain't even me, how could I ever fly?

Its like trying to run in the standard boot size

When I need special quirks and works to make my life

feel like artwork.

After I'm finally me, the ferryman tells me to find an

anchor

Cause even if I'm me, I can still float to unwanted places

So I fly high and fly low looking here and there for

something to keep me down,

Money doesn't keep me down…

My everyday hobbies don't keep me down…

Nothing chained to this world can anchor me down.

I failed

I failed...

I crawl back with my head down low back to the

ferrymens home

It was the middle of the night, with stars shining real

bright just how he likes

Knock knock

. . .

Knock Knock

. . .

"Mr. Ferrymen?" I shout out

. . .

The night so silent I could hear Mrs. Moons spout

BANG BANG

Silence...

BANG

Silence...

The ferryman's, dead...

That morning his daughter and sister came to burn him,

and burn him we did,

We shared stories of his life and grieved for the world

now without his kindness.

"He gave me my life ba-" I stutter

He was my friend,

My family,

Not by blood but by heart,

He was my souls healer,

He was my anchor...

But now I must let him become the light house for my journey,

"May your light guide me to my people." We set fire to his gentle body

May we all find our anchors in life that keep us steady in the storms

May we all find our lighthouses that guide us through the waters

May we all find our fleet, our people, to support us through the hard days and long nights

Most live without living, so find the things and people that give you the breath to *live* life.

Find your breath, find your life, find your you, and *live*!

Thank you. . .

Thank you. . .
What a powerful phrase. . .
So. . .

Thank you. . .
Thank you to my teasing mom who sacrificed her life.
Thank you for doing the hard things,
even when it wasn't asked for.
Thank you for doing the small things,
that went without a wink.
Thank you, for being my personal doctor, lawyer,
encourager, supporter, teacher, chef, driver, fighter,
cleaner ,and most of all, my mother.
I know you said you love me to the moon and I'd never
win, but my chem teacher had said nothing beats 6.02 x
10^{23}, so I love you 6.02 x 10^{23}, so ya beat that.
Thank you. . .

Thank you. . .
Thank you to my wild Dad who sacrificed his life.
Thank you for doing the boring things that nobody else
wanted, just to keep the peace.

Thank you for doing the fun things,

that set me on all my hobby paths.

Thank you for working to get money, for working to

make us happy, for working for a better life that nobody

coulda' asked for.

I know you said life's hard work on my car rides to work,

and you're right, so thank you for your hard work, even if

it was just for those two specific skylanders.

Thank you. . .

Thank you. . .

Thank you to my sister Caylinn who taught me about life.

Thank you for your life, your brightness through the

darkness.

Thank you for your experience, shining a light on some

of life's demons.

Thank you for all the times in life where sometimes it

needed some shining, for all the times in life you shined

a light on some people, for all the times you shined your

light in some corners for your brother.

I know you said I'm a frog, and I know I said you are

too, but let's both be real for a quick second, we're both

Salmons swimming up our own streams aspiring to be
our own King's and Queen's.
Thank you. . .

Thank you. . .
Thank you to my sister Cali who brought a part of me to
light.
Thank you for your seriousness, teaching me there are
hard lines and how to not cross.
Thank you for your goofiness, teaching me I'm not alone
and it's okay to weird out
Thank you for your quirks and specialty, showing me
sometimes we need custom sizes to feel like artwork,
cause we are all beautiful pieces.
Thank you. . .

Thank you. . .
Thank you to my sister Cici who is growing up, showing
me, me, from a third point view.
Thank you for your perspective, not only in third point
view, but within your slaying comebacks.
Thank you for your personality, always singing your
glowin' confidence.
Thank you for adding the cherry to our family's ice

cream, like the star upon a christmas tree,

you miss, slay.

Thank you. . .

Thank you. . .

It's such a powerful phrase.

We all want to feel it but never say it.

So thank you to the world, because Thank you isn't a

holiday, it's an action.

So who else may I thank

Thank you. . .

But I'm not done yet. . .

Thank you. . .

Thank you to Kayla, my light in the dark.

Thank you for standing by me no matter the Storm.

Thank you for being my anchor, pulling me out of the

dark.

Thank you for being kind, clever, beautiful both inside

and outside, mine, quick-witted, generous, loving, pure,

hardworking, a candle in my abyss, smart, and perhaps

one day even more.

I know you said you love me, and I know,

but I loved you first.

Thank you. . .

Thank you. . .

Thank you to Storm, my baby girl,

who chose me in my trial.

Thank you for your sassy attitude from when you walked

to how you talked.

Thank you for your love,

if only as a year long gift from god.

Thank you for your love, sass, the times we played hide

and seek, fetch, tug of war, and with the blue ball, for

your cuddles, for your protection, for your storm.

I know I've said it a thousand times over,

but I love you baby girl,

and there's not one dog that could replace even your

ashes...

I love you, thank you. . .

Thank you. . .

Thank you to the supporters in my life.

Thank you for your kindness, Thank you for your love.

Thank you for the time that you have given up.

Thank you, Brandon and Shaniese and Miss Stephanie

for the opportunity you've given all of us, Thank you to all my teachers that gave me the time of day, Thank you to past friends for supporting me along the way, Thank you to Matt and April for inviting me over just to learn and bond, Thank you god for all the blessings you've sent my way – I appreciate you even if I fail to say it every day – Thank you for the people in my life that have supported me along the way.
I know it's been claimed as "not a problem" but truly, thank you.
Thank you. . .

Thank you. . .
Thank you all for giving me the time of day
Thank you for your candles in an otherwise dark hallway
Thank you for adding your ships to the fleet and guiding me along the way
Thank you, it's such a powerful phrase. . .
Thank you. . .

Acknowledgements

Thank you Brandon, for giving me this amazing opportunity to start my published writing journey. I truly appreciate the time, effort, and care you put into every Saturday and Wednesday workshop—it has given me the boost to begin swimming up a new river in life. Thank you, Shaniese, for the weekly updates and reminders, and for taking this journey with us, writing knockout-level poems that inspire us every time you present. A big thank you to Emily, who took the time to create the cover and help edit and format the book. It's been a pleasure working with you, and I appreciate every second you've devoted to helping us all. Thank you Miss Stephanie for helping and reminding us all of who we are, without that we are simply an abyss breathing without living, thank you. And thank you to all the speakers during this camp that have boosted our experiences.

Last but certainly not least, I'd like to thank everyone in my life who supports me every step of the way. Thanks, Mom and Dad, for loving and pushing me every day. Thanks, Kayla, for lifting me up with your kind heart and delicious Butterfinger drop-offs when I'm facing my bears. Thank you to my sisters for helping and inspiring me to grow as a person… I guess. Just kidding—I love you guys. Thank you to the teachers who supported me and helped me grow, making some of the hardest times in life just a little bit brighter. And finally, thank you to my baby Storm, who only came into my life for a little over a year but was the best first dog I could have ever bonded with and you helped me through the hardest time in my life. I love you, girl. Rest in peace.

About the Author

Cyle Salmon is a young author striving for the gold in his life, not from the world but from himself. He's been going through the mountains, sharks, and bears throughout his life with each year bringing new challenges. But through his determination and the people around him he's gotten through his countless trials with love and new found perspective. This book marks the beginning of his journey not only as a published author but as a dreamer who now knows how possible those dreams are. His writing invokes a mythical feeling and a need for greatness through heated lines, to slow and fearful moments fueled with raging emotions. When he's not working on his world of creativity on paper, he's always cooking something up in his river for the world to one day see. For the world it's a book, for him it's his whole life and more.

youthwriterspress.com

A program of Youth Writer's Camp, Inc., Youth Writer's Press exists to create a safe space where young voices are heard, valued, and amplified. We are dedicated to producing and publishing work that allows youth to share their truths with the world. Our mission is to equip the next generation of writers with the resources, confidence, and platform to turn their stories into lasting works that resound far beyond the page.

youthwriterscamp.com

This book was created as part of Youth Writer's Camp, Inc., a nonprofit organization whose mission is to motivate communities to redefine hope for young people through mentoring, enrichment, and creativity.

In our workshops and programs, we blend literacy enrichment, social-emotional development, and creative entrepreneurship — using writing as a tool for healing, growth, and community connection.

Youth Writer's Camp Values:

COURAGE Creating the strength to face challenges with confidence.

RESILIENCE Creating the ability to bounce back and keep moving forward.

EMPATHY Creating connections by truly understanding others' feelings.

AUTHENTICITY Creating a space where you can be your true self without masks.

TRANSPARENCY Creating an atmosphere of openness and honesty, where vulnerability is valued.

ENTERPRISING Creating opportunities through innovation and a dynamic mindset.